DENIZEN

Poems & Conversations

ROBERT HOGFOSS

DENIZEN
POEMS & CONVERSATIONS

iUniverse books may be ordered through booksellers or by contacting:

iUniverse
1663 Liberty Drive
Bloomington, IN 47403
www.iuniverse.com
844-349-9409

ISBN: 978-1-6632-3958-7 (sc)
ISBN: 978-1-6632-3959-4 (e)

Print information available on the last page.

iUniverse rev. date: 01/13/2023

CONTENTS

I. Poems 1

Seems Like Years Go By, I Never Notice 3
Let Me Tell You of the Morning 4
Seven Sisters in the Seven Devils Mountains 5
Traveling Spring 7
Returning Home 9
Late Morning 10
All Last Week 11
These Few Words 12
The Long Red Twilight 13
Through the Woods 14
Wisdom of the Ranch Hands 15
Perhaps We Should All Bind Our Mistakes So Close 16
The Woods by the River 17
First of December 18
Time Passes 19
November Moon 20
On Your 33d Birthday 21
Moonlight and Memory 22
Written in Moonlight 23
Revision 24
Like Stepping into A Canoe 25
One Hundred Years from Now 27
The Perfect Code 28
I Purge All the References to Sadness 29

Would We Have Done Anything Different 30

Walking into the Open.. 31

To My Children and My Children's Children 33

I Am the Wind... 35

After Rain 36

Carry This... 37

The Only Wealth You Will Ever Need... 38

Letter from a Buddhist Monk... 39

Post tenebras, spero lucem... 40

If You Come Visit... 41

Words from My Father In a Dream 42

The Source... 43

Nothing To Be Done.. 44

How Long.. 45

Fireflies in Twilight.. 46

Consider the World as It Is... 47

Why Moonrise is the Subject of More Poems than Moonset................. 48

Memory 49

II.   Conversations 51

Conversations with the Earth Spirits 53

I
POEMS

SEEMS LIKE YEARS GO BY, I NEVER NOTICE

four black ravens
over the canyon
gliding no wind
in the trees

LET ME TELL YOU OF THE MORNING

Beginning to understand the importance
of what must be left out. Emptiness fills
the form; silence holds the message.

Let me tell you of the morning.
Moonlight and snow clouds
wind from the North.

SEVEN SISTERS IN THE SEVEN DEVILS MOUNTAINS

(after the Nez Perce myth of the Pleiades)

cold winter
mountains
long winter
hair all greasy
and already
I smell like bear

came up here
wandering
working through it
now I'm stuck
nobody else

roll over
squeaking hips
on snow
looking at
the stars

those six
up there
all clustered
whispering
and their sister

there but
hard to see
pulling night
across her face
so ashamed she left
and gave up loving me

TRAVELING SPRING

Clouds form over open ground
on warm days, then
      drift with the wind.
           I move on.

Sleep along the road. Stars bright.
Night clear.
Moving again before dawn.
Chasing prairie cloud shadows.

Warm wind from the Southwest. Spent six
days in the Bad Lands. "Mauve Terres."
Mako Sica. Ran the grassland along the
canyon rim every day. Camped by a small
water hole in Cottonwood and Juniper with
a Northern Shrike and Magpies. Antelope
slipping down to the water at night: faint
      tracks on the dry earth.

Camping in the Northern Rockies. Walking
through miles of Beargrass, up valleys and
cross country through the Subalpine Fir and
alpine flowered fields. Staying just now in
a small cirque on a rock ledge above a still
frozen lake. While writing this I notice that
my hands are perfumed from brushing back
      flowers on the path all morning.

Lonely beauty in the quiet. Cold
winds rushing
        all around.

I keep on traveling. On the edge of spring
for six weeks now. Five hundred Snow Geese
lifted up at dawn this morning from the refuge
where I'm camped, circled the thawing marsh and
then slowly settled down again. Testing the air,
sensing the still, frozen country to the North.

Flathead Valley cold.
Bison in their winter fur,
red calves fresh on wobbling legs.

RETURNING HOME

Returning home for a visit
long days driving across the
winter flatland. I feel like a
river running down to the sea
fanning out and slowing.

Over the years I have learned
that I feel strongest in the
mountains and dense forest.
Yet this flatland is a country
that still I know so well,

a country where the internal
landscape can also take on
an immense dimension.
At dusk I enter the woodlands
near home, my heart swirled by

many thoughts. I notice that
I have been holding my
shoulders back, my head up
all day. Night comes on, and
my eyes are filled with light.

LATE MORNING

Late morning. Still dark.
Black bottomed clouds moving
over the ridge, blowing through
the dark blue blackberry bushes.

I rise, night fog lifting up
from under leaves, through grass
rising with the color of ground
through breaks in cloud that bathe

the berry bushes all in light.

ALL LAST WEEK

All last week low clouds flying through valleys
up to Bear Springs. This week rains continue, and

     suddenly fire season's done.

I move on, picking apples in the Hood River Valley
before going back to school and work in town.

Winter sun. Valley in fog.
The apples so cold, hands numb,
     fumbling always
         dropping fruit.

THESE FEW WORDS

This winter still working in the woods, clearing.
land, bucking logs; splitting firewood for the
wealthy homes in Portland. Right now I sit in
my cabin, day tired in the growing dusk, too
worn to fix food, too restless to sleep.

My thoughts go back over the years. I think
of Colleen, and the women I've known in my
life. I think of Cory, driving cross country to
Idaho, to Colorado, to Texas and beyond. I
remember waking on the ground, covered by
frost, her eyelids jewels in first light. I remember
Heidi pulling me out of bed to stand at the window
and breathe in rich musk smells of spring on
North Albina Street. The girl in Norway kissing
me on the tram into Oslo, then disappearing in
the crowd at the night station. Chicago nights,
Seattle, dancing with Nahleen, born in China,
her black hair hanging down below her waist.

Last night I watched two deer wade the East Fork
in starlight, their fur glistening wet. Today
I saw a single Osprey circle low over the Bull Run
eyes sharp in the wind. Tonight I sit alone
with just my thoughts
          and these few words.

THE LONG RED TWILIGHT

Been working in the woods near ten years now.
When I began this work the log trucks I would
see rolling down from the hills carried only
three logs to a load, sometimes one. Now they
go by loaded with seven or nine stems to a truck.
Fallers moving further into the high country;
old growth hunted out from all the good ground.

In the spring and fall when there are no wildfires
burning we light the slash left dead and down
in the clear cuts. Swathes and patches of bare
ground skinned out from the hide of the old hills,
the earth left raw; smoke belching up from the
high leads and log trucks pulling up the grade,
like smoke from the rendering fires, where the
hunters gather round with their fleshing knives
as the bones pile up all around, in the long red
       twilight that stretches
          across the West.

THROUGH THE WOODS

High clouds over the west ridge
again this morning. Crisp air.
Short days. Fire season done.
Next week most the crew heads back
to school, or back to work in town.

I've been to school and I've been
to town. Not sure where I'm going now…

Just looking for the
      the right cut in the trees
          the light falling on the trail;

    through the woods

      and gone.

WISDOM OF THE RANCH HANDS

Sometimes it's so foggy back the mountain
you can't see tomorrow.

*

If you drink you're like to get drunk.
It takes money to drink and time to get drunk
and we ain't got neither.

*

The past is nothing.
It's the present and the future that'll kill you.

PERHAPS WE SHOULD ALL BIND OUR MISTAKES SO CLOSE

My dog Sourdough gets into the chicken
coop on the ranch, and kills a good egg
laying bird. Justin quietly ties the dead
bird firmly to Sourdough's neck, and tells
me we must leave it there for a week.

The first day Sourdough is proud of her
new possession. Second day she tries
desperately to shake it free. For the rest
of the week she lays motionless and
mournful, with her increasingly
        unwelcome companion.

I feel sorry for the dog, but it works.
She never goes near the chickens again.
Perhaps we should all bind our mistakes
so close to ourselves, until we
      so loathe the burden
          that we learn.

THE WOODS BY THE RIVER

Cottonwood, Elm samara,
samaras of Ash, Maple,
float in the blue dusk air.
Seeds of the tree flesh, hard
roots grown tall, dropping
seed to the grasses, sifting
down the gentle breeze to
settle in with the rich moist
earth, spice smell of earth.
Thinking of you, my dear, as
I walk the woods by the river.

FIRST OF DECEMBER

First of December and snow is moving down
from the hills like a wary tenant long displaced
moving down by night, like some old guerilla
band returning and remembering
      the terrain by its feel.

Every morning just at dawn we lift off from
the Air Base by the river; helicopters rising
through the fog and sunlight, the earth
slipping by me through the
windowed cockpit, radios chattering
in my headset,
      sun warming the flight helmet.

In the dawn light I realize that
I have never been so happy.
The city is cold but the
mountains shine. Raven and
Elk stand out from 10,000 feet,
clear sky all around. In the crater
of the volcano the winds are
kicking up old ash, swirling
dark bands through the
      white new fallen snow.

TIME PASSES

Time passes. Sitting in the winter wind
drinking new red wine, reading Neruda and
Vallejo in the Spanish. Nursing aches and
heartaches and all these memories from the
   years gone by.

I look out to the mountains in the West,
where snow is falling gently on the
dark green trees in the distance,

  and I wonder

    where this road will lead me next.

NOVEMBER MOON

we let go the oars
on outgoing tide, drifting
clouds across the moon

ON YOUR 33D BIRTHDAY

Green canyon walls rush past
these last four days, as I float
this wild river. The river is
always the same, yet always new.

We are now on a lake. Paddling
along, I think of you on this day,
across vast mountains and green
forests, as you begin another year.

You worry your life has been too
meandering. On his 33d birthday
the poet Tu Fu looked back, and
wished he would've raised melons,

yet it is his words we remember
today, after all these years. So
raise melons if you must, but still
find time to meander and make art.

MOONLIGHT AND MEMORY

The canals are cold this time of year
and the fields of flowers lay fallow.
The banks of the Zeider Zee are
always green, though, always firm.

Across the ocean, through the years
and through the vines of daughters and
granddaughters, a bouquet of tulips lays
waiting next to an opened bottle of wine.

Light from a full moon fills two empty
glasses. A man walks out of a quiet
room, his heart filled with memories.

WRITTEN IN MOONLIGHT

Our history was written in
moonlight, but light fades
as distance grows, and
time apart is a distance
measured, so we carried
the light within, where
time and distance have no
measure, and where we
would always be together.

REVISION

First Draft

Three thousand miles,
three thousand days,
never seemed too much.
Only love lasts forever.

Revised Draft

Three thousand miles,
three thousand days,
never seemed too much
　　…until it was.

LIKE STEPPING INTO A CANOE

That's how Billy Collins describes
the act of moving from the title of
a poem to the poem itself, from
firm ground to something buoyant.

I love this image of transition, and
of tension between the name of a
thing and the thing itself. But I
must admit that I forget the names

of most poems I have read, like
one forgets the distant shore long
departed, your eyes instead
following the graceful lines of

the gunwales curving upward
toward the bow, where little
waves slap gently against the
drum tight skin of the canoe

saying softly, again and again
that some things need no names.

Poetry and music and love can
all leave you equally unmoored
drifting further and further
toward the middle of the lake

where the reflections of the clouds
exist apart from the clouds themselves
and where you no longer recall
the name of that place you left.

ONE HUNDRED YEARS FROM NOW

One hundred years from now
as you sleep beneath this tree
if they count backward through
the rings of time, they will sense
the fragrance of this one sun
dappled moment, as the tree
       breathes in your scent.

THE PERFECT CODE

I am being searched for desperately.
Some officials want my help, saying
a new code is impossible to break,
that it is a matter of national security.

I agree to listen, but then shake
my head. I tell them that code is
like language, like music; random
symbols only become decipherable

when two or more people agree on
the interpretation. The perfect code,
I tell them, is the one that is not shared:
            the voice of a lonely man.

I PURGE ALL THE
REFERENCES TO SADNESS

I purge all the references to sadness in my
journals, then laugh out loud when I realize
that it doesn't make me feel better. I save
only this:

There is a sadness sometimes too deep
to understand. There are days that I have felt this.
There are years that I have not understood.

WOULD WE HAVE DONE ANYTHING DIFFERENT

Would we have done anything different had
we known it was the last time we would meet?
Would we have lingered longer, relishing the
sense of touch and scent, looked more clearly
into each other's eyes? Or would we deny that
such things could ever change, much less end.

If you could know the future would you try to
change it, or would you let your heart remain
in the moment, understanding that
        the end is already here and waiting.

WALKING INTO THE OPEN

Senior representatives of all trees are gathered
on the gently sloping hillside, facing south. I
am asked to speak to them. It is a beautiful
sunny day; blue skies and gentle breeze.

I turn to all the flowering trees, the Angiosperms,
on my right. <I am glad to see you here>, I say.
<You are welcome here. You have made yourselves
known by seeking new paths. You have made friends

with the insects and with the spectrum of light, and
you have thrived. You are willing to bend and to
move, and you have done well. You are opportunistic,
seeking light and food and sex where you can find it,
but that is good: that is your way.>

Then I turn to my left, to the conifers, the
Gymnosperms. They are standing tall and proud.
<Welcome>, I say. <You have been here long,
and you are patient. Your spirit is simple, but strong.

You have stood fast as the world and stars and all
living things around you have changed. You remain
strong, and the wind remains your strongest ally.
You are aspirational, and that is good: that is your way.>

The trees sway in the breeze. The sound from the
Angiosperms is light and melodic. The sound from
the Gymnosperms is a low, steady hum. I walk down
the hillside, between the groups of trees. I sense all
sorts of four legs and two-legs and winged spirits

at the margins of the hillside. I walk out into the open,
seeking my own light, and sensing much of that within.

TO MY CHILDREN AND MY CHILDREN'S CHILDREN

To my children and my children's children:
now and again you should spend a day alone
out of doors in a place you love, observing
      the ways of the world in silence.

Like this day. It is perfect fall migration
weather, so I load a day pack and walk
into the Conboy Wildlife Refuge before
dawn, intent to sit and watch the rhythms
of this place, from sunrise to sunset. I settle
among some willows by a pond at daybreak.
Over the course of the day I feel the changes
in the wind and light, the movement of
      the birds and insects.

A family of beavers is building a dam on the
pond, and after many hours of sitting, a young
beaver grows comfortable enough with my
presence that he begins to cut the willows only
ten feet from where I sit. He carefully cuts the
stems at forty-five degree angles, then peels and
sizes them into two-foot lengths and dives under
water to plant them in the mud for winter food.

In the middle of the afternoon the young beaver
drags a fresh cut willow across my legs, then
      pauses to consider me.

I wonder if he knows, at some genetic level, how
his *Castor canadensis* forebearers drew the trappers
out West, how they opened the door to the hordes
of *Homo sapiens*, John Colter leaving the Lewis
and Clark expedition on its return trip back down

the Missouri, to join trappers coming upstream to
explore the mountain west, and feed the demand
for beaver hats and furs in England and the East.

The young beaver concludes his assessment of
me and dives back down below the pond. No
thought of history or fashion. No worries about
the lone and motionless human on the shore
         who is threatening no one
                  this time.

I AM THE WIND

I am the wind that presses
down the hemlock at timberline.

I am the edge of the meadow.
I am the day you walk in cloud forests.

I am the sleep you find on sky islands.
I am the hillside made of aspen

where my roots become myself.
I am the arrivada; the massing of

sea turtles in moonlight tide, and
I am the light behind your eyes.

AFTER RAIN

After rain. Wet smell earth. Time in quiet.
Once I saw a full ditch dark and late, after
rain, up to the level edge of road with fireflies.

Fire flies. Lightning to the north.
Summer. Yellow Medicine. Long ago,

…longing.

CARRY THIS

I am in an outdoor amphitheater, filled with people.
It feels partly like a concert and partly like an academic
colloquium. Suddenly, the Dalai Lama comes up to me

and hands me a small, gray leather pouch, with a leather
strap. I open it. Inside are eight small wooden rectangles,
old and weathered wood, light tan in color, connected by

a leather strap. The Dalai Lama asks me to care for the
bag and its contents for a while. I put the wood pieces
back in the leather bag, and put the bag around my neck

tucking it inside my shirt. The Dalai Lama smiles.
Several monks become distressed, and other people
nearby are clearly upset. The Dalai Lama turns to them

and asks whether they would rather carry the bag and
the eight pieces of wood. They all say yes, desperately.
'That is why you cannot,' says the Dalai Lama.

THE ONLY WEALTH YOU WILL EVER NEED

The only wealth you will ever need appears
on a sun filled Tuesday afternoon in early spring
when thousands of cherry blossoms let loose and
flutter in the wind, brushing against your face and
filling curbs along the streets, piling up in small
drifts against the walls and houses where you live.

No one seems to understand that here is the beauty
you should see, that this is the only wealth you will
ever need. But children see more than adults, and
children are playing in the blossom filled gutters,
tossing handfuls of flowers in the air, the petals
falling lightly back to earth as blessings on us all.

LETTER FROM A BUDDHIST MONK

Turn and face your
real enemies:
ambition
violence
hatred
greed.

Lines from a letter received by a friend's parents in Viet Nam long ago. I found out recently the lines were from a poem called 'Condemnation,' written in 1964 by Thich Nhat Hanh, a Vietnamese Buddhist monk. Thich was labeled anti-war because of the poem, and not allowed back to Viet Nam until 2005, when he returned to his monastery in Hue. He passed away in 2022 at age 95.

POST TENEBRAS, SPERO LUCEM

(after a son returns from serving as a combat medic in Iraq)

After darkness, I hope for light.
But I am Job. I am Ayyub.
Descendant of Esau.

There is no light. My son
drank the dark water of the
Euphrates, still dying of thirst.

Elihu listened. My friends listened,
but no one could explain why God
uses the Adversary. Why evil exists.

God destroys the innocent
and the wicked together.
Thus said Aristotle. But

ten children gone, ten returned.
Not the same, God. If I cursed
your name, would it be any different?

I choose to curse the Adversary.
I curse the darkness, God, and in
this darkness, I still pray for light.

Spero lucem.

IF YOU COME VISIT

I live alone in a stone house by a
river. My neighbors are eagles and
deer. Our companion is the wind.

I no longer want to see cities. I am
not comfortable wearing green robes.
I am not here by dharma transmission.

I am just an old man with a long past.
I rise before the sun. I walk the hills along
the river by day. I sit under the full moon.

If you come visit
you will not find me.

WORDS FROM MY FATHER IN A DREAM

It is good to want less.
Better to need less. That
is what makes us strong.

THE SOURCE

All of the water on earth is
more celestial than we think.
It came not from the clouds
but from the stars.

NOTHING TO BE DONE

I sit on high rocks above a wide river.
I have been living here for years now.
The wind and eagles bring me news.

Why would I return to live among people
racing to work and to worry, when
there is so much nothing to be done.

HOW LONG

How long have I lived
in this stone house in the
mountains by a river?

When I was young, I spent
my summers in adventure and
winters in the universities.

Now I live alone. My
neighbors are the quail,
the hawks and the eagles.

I was married once, raised
children in large cities and
worked in tall buildings.

Now I rise every morning
in the dark and watch the
morning light and wind.

I watch the sun rise and the moon
set. I watch the stars move over
the sky every night, the world

spinning through cold space.
How long have I lived in this
stone house by the river?

FIREFLIES IN TWILIGHT

this life but an instant
all life but a moment
hovering over the falling tide
fireflies in twilight

CONSIDER THE WORLD AS IT IS

moist air rises from the green
forest bright clouds bloom in
afternoon raindrops fall on this
blue planet bright eyes all

WHY MOONRISE IS THE SUBJECT OF MORE POEMS THAN MOONSET

Poets rarely speak of moonset,
finding the muse more readily
in the fullness of early evening.

Perhaps it is too much drink or
song too early in the evening,
too little patience, or just that

inspiration occurs more often
in the arrival of things than in
their passing. Or just tradition.

I rarely see the moon rise in
this deep river gorge where
I live, but moonset here can

be beautiful. The canyon walls
reach high behind me, but the
river opens to the west, where

the moon can expand as it sets.
Like right now, as one thousand
geese fly by me low, framed by

the full moon setting. The sound
of their calls and wings fill the air,
while everyone around me sleeps.

MEMORY

You are alive right now in someone else's memory.
You have no control over this. You have simply
been summoned.

You cannot be sure where you are in this other person's
memory. You cannot know your age or what you are doing.

It is not your memory.

You have little control of your own memory in any event, as
it drifts and fades over time.

Memories are made of fabric that we weave and
re-weave on remembrance.

Remembrances of a shared event are never exactly the same.
They never will be the same.

Even as you read these words your memory of things has begun to fade
and change.

Remember this.

II

CONVERSATIONS

CONVERSATIONS WITH THE EARTH SPIRITS

In the time of pandemic many of us were dreaming more than usual, and many remembered their dreams more than usual. I learned how to remember dreams as a volunteer at the University of Chicago sleep lab many years ago, and I learned how to be aware of and have some control in dreams (lucid dreaming). My dreams took on an added dimension during the pandemic, though, bringing me to long encounters with HuldreFolk -- the earth spirits held in respect by my family and Scandinavian peoples generally (these earth spirits exist around the world, but are known by different names).

I never had such a long series of linear dreams on the same theme as have been these dreams with the earth spirits, and I never had dreams with such long conversational dialogues. But here we are. The following are some notes from these strange encounters, which are still ongoing. These dreams helped me survive the pandemic and restored a sense of gratitude for the natural world around us.

I have only committed some of these dreams to written word, but I will keep trying, and I will keep adding to these notes as it goes. It is easier to remember dreams than it is to write them down, though, because as the HuldreFolk tell us dreams are wispy things, not easy to capture.

For the first several weeks after the pandemic caused lockdowns worldwide, I dreamt only of traveling, in the form of walking. Every night, in dreams, I was walking. Sometimes I was walking on a high mountain trail. Other times I walked among abandoned cars on freeways, or through empty city streets. No sense of destination, no clear point of departure. Just traveling by walking, every night.

One night when I was on a mountain trail in dreams, wondering how long I would just keep wandering, HuldreFolk suddenly surrounded me. They said they had come to take me underground with them for a while. Our Norwegian grandmother Elise told us about HuldreFolk when we were little, and I am convinced she showed them to me then. Grandma Elise lived in an old log house that had a pump handle in the kitchen, connected to her water well. She was proud of that pump, because it was almost the only evidence of modern life in her log house. So when the washbasin near the sink was full Elise would carry it outside to dump out. But every time she did that, before pouring the water out, she would sing a little song asking the HuldreFolk to move away so the wash water would not surprise them or get them wet.

Grandma Elise did not speak English, but gestures from her and help from our father explained things (this gap in communication encouraged me years later to learn Norwegian, something our parents did not teach their children, wanting us to become assimilated in America). Grandma Elise believed that the HuldreFolk were little beings that lived under and protected the earth, and who helped bring balance and luck to your life (or the opposite if you offended them). It amounted to showing respect for the earth around you; consideration and respect for all things living near you. I always loved the idea of the HuldreFolk, but they never visited me in dreams before this.

*

I stayed with the HuldreFolk in my dreams for weeks, which then became months. I learned many things from them, starting with a better understanding of who they were and what they did. They told me that unlike Grandma Elise's description, they really did not live *under* the earth, but *in* the earth…in the hills and trees and rivers and rocks. Thus they were able to see all things going on above ground. They also explained that in fact they did not really affect your luck – good or bad – but simply reflected it. So if you did something that harmed the earth you would suffer consequences. Likewise, if you were considerate about the earth you would gain good fortune and happiness. In either case the effect had the appearance of luck, good or bad, but it was really a reflection of your own action, without interference by any other entity. I later learned that the HuldreFolk were being a bit disingenuous about their ability to influence things in this initial discussion, but it was a nice introduction.

*

During another night of dreams the HuldreFolk told me they thought humans did not touch the earth enough anymore, that we had so insulated ourselves through buildings and cars and concrete that we had lost an essential connection. They were especially bothered by roads, saying that if people did not move so fast and far without touching the earth they would find more balance in their lives and with the world.

They suggested that perhaps I could help get people out of houses and cars and concrete buildings more often, to get back in contact with the earth. I told them that would be difficult because humans like their luxuries, and I had little ability to influence large numbers of people in any event. I also asked about their preoccupation with roads, surprised that they were not more concerned about fossil fuel use generally, since that was a more common concern in today's world. The HuldreFolk were puzzled by that question and asked me more about fossil fuel. I did not know the exact answers to all of their questions, so they asked me to research it. Amazingly, when I awoke the next morning I went to the computer to do research, as requested by the HuldreFolk.

*

The next night I reported to the HuldreFolk that oil is indeed used primarily for transportation (cars, trucks and airplanes). I told them that although coal was used for transportation last century, it has more recently been used for electric generation, but even that is now being replaced by natural gas, wind and solar. Given the prevalence of fossil fuel use in modern life and the fact that more than half of all oil is used for transportation in one form or another, I expected the HuldreFolk would immediately focus on fossil fuels generally, or oil specifically, as their primary concern. But they remained nonplussed, saying transportation other than walking was the major reason people were increasingly disconnected from the earth. That was cause for their concern. They said it would make no difference if someone was driving an electric car or living in a solar powered house if they rarely left the car or abode to touch the earth. I found that to be an interesting point. Not exactly consistent with current thought, but interesting. I later learned that their concern and emphasis on transportation by walking was just meant to be illustrative of their larger theme, one of slowing down and living more lightly on the earth.

*

I pressed the HuldreFolk further about climate change one night, telling them that human activities were adding carbon to the atmosphere, through activities involving transportation, but also land clearing, agriculture, raising animals, etc. They acknowledged all of that but kept a focus on roads and getting people back in touch with the earth itself. First things first, they said.

*

Some nights later I asked the HuldreFolk what they thought of the pandemic. To my surprise, they seemed generally aware of it, but uninterested. They liked the fact that it had so markedly reduced transportation, and that more people were walking outside, but the disease itself and all the suffering and death associated with it did not seem to bother them significantly. When I asked them about that, they said birth and death are all just part of a circle, and that neither should be a worry or concern. I said that seemed a bit cavalier, and that I would have expected them to care more about suffering if they care so much for the earth. They said they did care about suffering, but since no one can avoid suffering and it is part of all life (not just human life), you can only do what you can for the living, while they are alive. I still thought that was more callous than I expected of them, and that in turn led to a long discussion. They said kindness to and compassion for the living while they are living is key (that and their dogged focus on less transportation generally, with more frequent recharge by walking on the earth).

The HuldreFolk said that humans tend to think of life (and time) as a river, always flowing but only in one direction. Once water passes a certain point it is thought to be gone. Water passed, and a life lived, was over to someone watching from the side. But the HuldreFolk explained that the river (and the lakes and the ocean) are all just part of a circle bringing water to the clouds and the clouds bringing rain back to ground. No life or death, no one direction. The hydrologic cycle their strong metaphor for life in general. They emphasized the importance of circles: our planet, the moon and sun, our orbit around the sun and our moon's orbit around us.

I asked the HuldreFolk if they die. There was some gentle laughter in the background, and they said of course we die, but we just continue in the circle, like you and everything else. It was clear that I was not likely to get a better explanation, so I moved on.

*

It occurs to me that I have been referring to the HuldreFolk as a single entity, which I guess they are to some extent, but let me explain. I am embarrassed to say was it was only after several weeks of these dreams that I asked the HuldreFolk if they were a single entity or not, since all this time there had been only one spokesperson for them but it seemed that there were always many present. There was gentle laughter again, almost like the sound of water in a brook in the background, but with some deeper notes added. I was told that there are a multitude of HuldreFolk, that they are everywhere just like us humans. Are you individuals, I asked, or just one entity. Of course we are individuals, they said, and of course we are one thing. Again, just like you. At this point I realized that they often spoke in riddles, or circles as they would prefer to say.

These convoluted conversations were becoming typical, but I persisted. Why do I feel like I have been talking with only one individual if there are so many of you, I asked. Again the faint laughter. Who do you want to talk to, was their response. And why can I not see you, I asked. Suddenly I was surrounded with creatures of varying size, similar to human form but different enough to be noticeable when encountered. I was startled, so one of the HuldreFolk said they do not often make themselves visible to humans because it really is just distracting, and that it's better to think of them as individual trees or rivers or lakes or rocks, because that is where they reside.

So are you everywhere, I asked. Everywhere there are trees and rivers and lakes and rocks they answered. Are there HuldreFolk in large cities, I asked. Yes, came the answer, but only where there are parks or gardens, large trees or water. That is part of our concern; when people gather in cities you increasingly tend to forget about the natural world, and that is when you lose the essential connection. Are there HuldreFolk in the sky, I asked. Of course, came the response, and suddenly I could see certain forms take shape out of clouds overhead. Why do I seem to hear only one voice when there are so many of you, I asked again. A large HuldreFolk instantly appeared before me, speaking in the voice I had become accustomed to, and said that was because I was most used to its particular manner, since it walks with me every day along trails where I live. Then other HuldreFolk voices chimed in greeting, some sounding literally like chimes and others, who were living in rocks, having deep voices spoken slowly.

We had a long conversation that night. I eventually said that I needed to get some rest…which meant I needed to awaken for a while.

*

Are you known as HuldreFolk everywhere, I asked one night. No, they said. Your family is from Norway. Many Scandinavians and Icelanders and those on the Faroe Islands know us as HuldreFolk, but peoples elsewhere have different names for us. Are you all the same, though -- I asked – wherever you are. Yes, but we take on different attributes depending on where we live, just like you. Traditional, village and rural peoples recognize us most easily, as earth spirits, which is what we are.

What about elves and fairies, I asked, are they different. The HuldreFolk said that elves and fairies are really just HuldreFolk, often young ones, but still earth spirits. What about trolls, I asked, are trolls also HuldreFolk. To this I heard outright laughter. No, they said; trolls are just your imagination.

*

During all this time I have been living alone on a small ranch in the rural West. I was a recluse before the pandemic, but once the lockdowns occurred I became an involuntary hermit. I had very little contact with any other human beings during the pandemic, and then only at a distance wearing masks. I asked the HuldreFolk if my isolation is what caused their visitation to me in my dreams. No, we have always been here, and always in your dreams, they said, but you are paying more attention now. Plus, it seemed like you needed company. I did, I said. Thank you.

*

On another night the HuldreFolk asked about my work as an environmental lawyer, and the discussion turned to the concept of Environmental Impact Statements (EISs) under the National Environmental Policy Act (NEPA), one of our oldest environmental laws. They were familiar with NEPA and EISs generally (not surprising, I suppose, because it was my dream they were in), and they were pleased that this was required for large projects. They understood that an EIS is intended to identify potential environmental impacts of large human actions, and to discuss a range of alternative actions, but they could not understand why the law did not require selection of the alternative with the least environmental impact. The law is procedural only, I explained. The process is intended to encourage discussion and consideration, to balance various goods and needs, I said, but it does not require a specific alternative. But why would anyone initiate an action if adverse impact to the earth has already been demonstrated, they asked. They had a good point, but I did not try to explain that it took tremendous effort just to get NEPA's procedural elements in place…we had not yet convinced enough people of the import of less environmental impact generally.

They pursued the topic, though, saying that in the long run actions with adverse environmental impacts cost more to humans than alternatives with lesser impact. People do not always (or even often) think long term, I said. But life is long term, the world is long term, said the HuldreFolk. People should see that bad decisions will visit their children and their children's children, if not themselves. People need to remember the value of slowing down, they said, of walking a trail instead of driving a road. Slowing down helps you think long term.

*

In dreams one night our discussions turned to whether and how often people have seen HuldreFolk. They said it depends on the person – and the mood of the local HuldreFolk – but that it is quite common. Are people glad to see you, I asked, or are they sometimes frightened. Again, it depends on the person, they said, and on whether the person is comfortable in nature or somewhat frightened by it. Are there any HuldreFolk who permanently live in forms visible to humans, I asked. Of course, they said. You have undoubtedly seen them. They may look a bit different, but they blend in well. They are gentle souls with great concern about the earth. Greta Thunberg is one of us, they said. That does not surprise me at all, I said. She is indeed different, but so impressive and such an inspiration for people. But she travels widely, I said, and I thought you were more local in residence. She does travel widely, they said, but she is from the Cloud People Clan (thus her overarching concern about global climate) and they all travel daily. You know other people who care greatly about the earth, said the HuldreFolk. Some of them are HuldreFolk, too. That also does not surprise me, I said, smiling and thinking of them.

*

Every night that the HuldreFolk visited me in dreams they emphasized their essential concerns. Be kind, they said. Touch the earth more often. Tell this to people, they said. Remember this.

*

A few nights later an elder HuldreFolk woman appeared to me, who I took as a shaman. She said I should recognize the importance of our exterior lives, the world around us. Do you mean other people, I asked. Yes, she said, but first focus on the actual world around you, the natural world. You have already done that more than you know, she said, and your memories reflect that. Bring up your most favored memories, in your dreams or in your waking life, and you will find that most of them involve or at least include the natural world that was around you when the memory was formed. Do this, she said: we were there when your memories were made, just like we are here now, in your dreams and in your waking world. Bring up some of your favored memories of the world around you over time. This will help you.

I am sitting in a canoe in the Boundary Waters Canoe Area of northern Minnesota. I am 16 years old (I know that because this was the first time I could drive myself there for a solo trip). I have made camp on a very small island in the middle of a large lake. Calm night, new moon, stars bright overhead. I light a stub of candle from my pack and set it on a rock by the shore, then paddle out into the completely calm lake. When I stop paddling to drift, I realize that the sky and the lake have become one…the stars are reflected in both. It is beautiful, but disorienting. I dip my paddle in the water and I see ripples in the sky. Fascinated, I forget about the time, then turn and see a small light in the distance. My candle that leads me home through the stars.

It is winter. I have come home to visit my parents in the North Country, and I take my part wolf dog with me on a winter camping trip to see a solar eclipse that will occur the next day. I tie a makeshift harness to the dog and let him pull me on my cross-country skis along the frozen river for miles, then find a useful snowdrift on the bank to make a camp. I hollow out the underside of the snowdrift and set up my sleeping bag in a large bivvy sack. After dinner my dog crawls into the bivvy at my feet, and we huddle through the sub-zero night. The next day I set up a small telescope to let the eclipsing sun shine against the snow.

Then we pack up and ski back down the long, frozen river in the moving shadows.

*

It is now late July, well into wildfire season where I live. I spent a decade between college and law school fighting wildfires, and I pay close attention to fire season. I have been maintaining a defensible fire perimeter around my house, mowing and clearing brush, setting up fire tanks, pumps and hose, and establishing evacuation procedures. With all that on my mind it is no surprise that my dreams took me to wildfires and firefighting, and no surprise that the HuldreFolk entered those dreams as well.

In my dream I asked them what they thought of wildfires and floods and storms…how did they react to such disasters. The HuldreFolk said that when such disasters are natural in cause it is simply a natural part of their existence. Some trees and plants and animals need abrupt change to reproduce and live. It is all part of the circle.

But what about disasters not natural in cause, those caused by humans, I asked, and what about climate change that is also caused by humans. There was a deep sighing, like wind in high branches, then a long pause. Finally, the HuldreFolk said that humans have always caused change, and the natural world itself is always changing, from rocks to plants to wind. But they understood that the impact from humans has become increasingly troublesome, that it disrupts the natural flow of the world.

Can you do something in response to human actions, I asked. If you can sometimes interfere in human actions involving roads and other things, can you not help reverse climate change, turn storms or wildfires. More wind in high branches, more sounds of sighing. The HuldreFolk eventually said that even though these human actions have been increasing and increasingly causing more damage to the natural world, they are in themselves part of the natural world. We can observe such large changes but we cannot interfere, they said. I was shocked at this and asked the HuldreFolk to explain. They went back to their discussions of circles within circles and how even circles change, and said that humans need to be responsible for their own change. When I awoke I found myself troubled by the dream.

*

Do HuldreFolk distinguish between good and evil, I asked one night. Of course, they said, to a large extent our purpose is to serve as a measure of good and evil. Evil is ignorance and hurt; good is kindness, knowledge and compassion. As we have told you before, they said, our role is largely to reflect human action, for good or for evil. I considered asking whether there are good and evil HuldreFolk, but thought better of it, worried that I might get the 'we reflect what we see' response.

*

I am camped on a plateau in the Upper Cathedral Lake Basin in the Pasayten Wilderness of the North Cascades in Washington State. It took me two days to get here from my truck parked at the Iron Gate trailhead. My wolf dog lays down next to me in a bivvy sack at night, then just before dawn we are awakened by rumbling in the earth. As we wonder at this sound, the rumbling becomes audible, and we lift up from where we lay just in time to see a herd of Bighorn Sheep go thundering past us, splitting to either side. Neither I nor my dog make any noise, just watch in amazement. Then we settle back down, feeling fortunate to be so right at home.

*

One night I dreamed of schools, of education, undoubtedly because that was prominent in the news and in my conscious mind. The government wanted schools to open but many teachers and parents were concerned about spread of the virus. I asked the HuldreFolk (who were, of course, lurking at the edges of the dream) if they had schools, if they knew how to read and write. I was immediately embarrassed after asking those questions, because the questions sounded more rude than I intended. There was a great deal of gentle laughter (a bit louder and longer than I thought necessary, but at least it was gentle). No, we do not have formal schools like you modern humans, came the answer. But we do believe strongly in education. We just do it a bit differently.

We tell stories, said the HuldreFolk. We tell our own stories and each other's stories, we tell the stories of our old ones. We watch, we listen. We teach our young what we see, and what we know. I was becoming increasingly embarrassed by my ignorance in the dream, having been with the HuldreFolk for months now, but I had to ask if they did indeed have young. No gentle laughter this time, but no rancor. Just a bit of awkward silence. Of course we have young, they said quietly. Just like you. You see young trees, even young rocks if you look around, do you not.

*

Another night in dreams I was surprised when the HuldreFolk asked me a question instead of the other way around. How do you feel about immigration, they asked. I realized that once again this was news from my waking world intruding on the dream, but I was taken aback by the topic, so I asked what they meant by the question. Well, we know that the issue of immigration bothers you humans often, especially of late, so we thought we should tell you what we think about it. Please do, I said.

We all come from somewhere else, they said. I looked skeptical and said that I understood and agreed that many peoples around the world have moved from one location to another, but not all, I said. Yes, given time, all come from somewhere else, they said. Start with the soil itself, they said: all soil has moved from the location of its parent material, by virtue of wind or water or time. And plants move, animals move. People too. Your own family moved from Norway to America, they said, not that long ago. Over time these things that move become 'naturalized' as humans say, but that only happens after they have moved. And they may move again.

What about weeds, I asked, invasive plants that are unwelcome and push out native forms. Like early Americans did with American Indians, they queried. I was taken aback again, both at the HuldreFolk's rather pointed question and on their knowledge of American history. But I pushed back, asking if they think weeds in the plant world are similar to colonization in the human world, that the force of occupation can ever justify itself. To my surprise, the HuldreFolk spokesperson paused, and said that yes, this is a point of considerable controversy among the HuldreFolk themselves. Gradual movement and migration is natural, they all agree, but forceful movements that displace existing plants or animals or people are not viewed with as much acceptance. Those who do accept it, however, think it is just part of the natural cycle of things. Like the circles you speak of so often, I asked. Yes, came the answer, but remember circles change, too.

*

I told the HuldreFolk shaman one night in dreams that I awoke disoriented that morning, unsure where I was or what day it was. She smiled. Sometimes being disoriented is helpful, she said. It reminds you to stay grounded, to stay present as you travel through life so you can find your way back when you stray too far, in waking life or in dreams. She then asked if once I was fully awake I knew where I was. Well, yes, I said, but it was confusing for a bit. Did you know what season it was, she asked. Yes, of course, I said. Did you know what part of day it was -- not the time of day -- but simply whether it was morning, afternoon or night. Yes, I said, I knew it was morning. What about the phase of the moon, did you recall whether it was a full moon or a new moon, waxing or waning. I thought a bit and said I hadn't considered that as I awoke, but now that you ask I do know that the moon is just after full, so it is waning. Well then, that is all the information you need to stay grounded, she said. You humans have become so obsessed with the precise time of day and day of week. Neither the planet nor any other living thing seeks to fragment reality so much as you do. Look to the natural rhythms and cycles of the world, it will help you relax.

She went on to tell me not to stay too long in memories, even the good ones. You have recalled some good memories in these 'lockdown' exercises, she said, and in itself that is good, because it has helped you in these difficult times. It will help you in any difficult time. But you cannot live only in past memories. So tell me what you saw today in your waking life, she said; what memory did you form today, from what was happening in the waking world. Well, I said, it was just an average day, there was nothing particularly memorable about it. Think harder she said, tell me what you saw...

> ...I saw Meadowlarks flying, I said, and I heard Meadowlarks singing. Much earlier in the season than usual, and that made me notice. I saw fresh deer and coyote tracks and scat. I saw some dug up ground that may have been from a badger, and I watched as a Swainson's Hawk caught a vole to eat....and I saw a large flock of Canada Geese heading north overhead, further evidence of an early spring.

That is good, said the elder HuldreFolk. That is all good. Far more than the 'nothing memorable' at your first recall. All things essential, worthy of perceiving, and memory. Now tell me of a memory that you think of often before falling asleep. I was a bit startled by that question, because there is one particular memory I often bring to mind while falling asleep...

> ...I have set up a small one-person tent and arranged my sleeping bag, pack and gear inside it. This is my favorite way to camp, traveling light and carrying everything I need on my back, with my little camp tucked among the trees leaving as little trace as possible. As I lay down in the tent and look at the stars, I think of those first pictures taken of earth from space, our blue marble planet at once alone and a part of the whole.

*

One night in a dream I met a human on the trail, who told me about a beautiful valley worth seeing. The human gave a specific compass direction to the valley from where we were. Then the person walked on, and I suddenly realized that I had no idea what direction that would be...I realized that I had never heard or asked about cardinal directions in dreams, relying instead on natural objects, the sun and the stars. A HuldreFolk appeared and confirmed that compass directions do not work in dreams, and that they are overly relied on by people in waking life. You know that the sun rises in the east and sets in the west, said the HuldreFolk, and you can tell north and south from the stars. What more do you need.

*

It is now Spring. The vernal equinox. The wildflowers are blooming, the grass greening and more and more birds and animals returning. The HuldreFolk were unsurprisingly joyous, acting in a festive mood every night in dreams. I asked them about it one night, remembering that there was no similar festive activity during the autumnal equinox or the winter solstice. We take joy in them as well, said the HuldreFolk, just as we take joy in the new moon and the full moon, in sunrise and sunset. But Spring is always special, a time of renewal, and it is for humans, too.

*

The next night the HuldreFolk said that they wanted to discuss time. That came from nowhere, I said, what do you want to say about time. Time is, they said. Time is what, I asked. Time just is, they said. I sighed, somewhat exasperated. So are you saying that time is part of a circle, I asked. Yes, they said. And no. Time just is.

OK, I said, 'time is,' but I expect you are aware that there is a past and a present and a future, and all of that 'just is,' too, but it does not help describe time as you do. This conversation started in the past, I said, and I expect you are about to answer, which is in the future. It does not seem to explain much to simply say that 'time is.' But those things are all the same, said the HuldreFolk. So are you espousing a Buddhist concept, I asked, that the 'now' is all that ever exists. Perhaps, they said, but we are not sure what you mean by the 'now'. I frankly doubted that answer, but I tried another tack. Do you think that at any point in time all space is fixed, but that any point in space all time is fluid, I asked. That is close to it, they said.

Or are you saying that time is just a circle, which seems to be your metaphor for everything, I asked. Yes...and no, came the answer. At this I said there was not much point in discussing it further, because they were just

speaking in riddles. OK, said the HuldreFolk. But let us do this again…
it will be both the same and different next time.

*

Several more weeks passed, then one night I found myself being escorted
by the HuldreFolk along one of my favorite trails, a loop trail in the Goat
Rocks Wilderness of Washington State. I was pleased to be walking this
beautiful trail with such esteemed companions, but it soon became evident
that they wanted to impart something to me.

You have been here before, said the HuldreFolk. Yes, I said, I have been
here many times over many years. You furthered someone's circle here
once, said the HuldreFolk. I stopped walking for a moment and paused.
Yes, I said…I deposited the ashes of a friend here once, a friend who was
struck down by cancer when young. You did that in an unusual way, said
the HuldreFolk. Yes, I said, surprised at how thoroughly the HuldreFolk
knew the details of my entire past, but even in the dream I realized that
they knew those details precisely because it was my dream.

Years ago I scheduled a helicopter flight while working with the Forest
Service to fly over this area in winter, I said, with the purported intent to
survey and count the Mountain Goat population (something that is done
periodically). The unofficial but real purpose, though, was to scatter a
friend's ashes from the air, since this was a place he loved.

What happened then, asked the HuldreFolk. Well, we brought the
helicopter to a hover over this beautiful glacial valley, I said, as the
HuldreFolk and I looked out over the valley. I opened the helicopter's
sliding plexiglass window to my left, held out the box of ashes and dumped
it. And what happened then, asked the HuldreFolk. The rotor wash from
the hovering helicopter was so strong, I said, that most of the ashes were
sucked up and into the intake vent for the jet turbine, which immediately
triggered engine chip alarms in the cockpit. The pilot and I worked to
assess and silent the alarms while looking for a safe place to make an
emergency autorotation landing if necessary. But there was no safe place
to land, was there, asked the HuldreFolk. No, there was no safe place to

land, I said. It was 'inhospitable terrain' as they say. It was, and is, a rugged place, which of course is why we all loved it.

We did recover power, I said, but it was a stressful situation. Life or death, said the HuldreFolk. I smiled, understanding the direction of their questions, and said…yes, that indeed was the theme of the day.

This place brings other memories, too, does it not, asked the HuldreFolk. I stopped walking again and thought, and then brightened and said yes, this is where I fought my very first wildfire, so many years ago. What about that, asked the HuldreFolk. Well, I said, we landed a helicopter on a ridge to the east, just outside the Wilderness boundary, and hiked down to work on a little lightning caused fire. Before the HuldreFolk could press another question I said that I knew…for some time I had known that wildfire policy back then was outdated and wrong…that the work we did on that little fire so many years ago left more scars on the landscape than did the fire, scars from digging fire lines and cutting up downed trees. I have visited that site before, I said. I visited it once with my sons, I said, and showed them that lesson.

One more remembrance, urged the HuldreFolk. I paused again to think, then said yes…I remember coming here by myself just before I moved my family to the East Coast to take my first full time job as a lawyer. I was apprehensive about leaving the American West, where I had lived for many years and a place I dearly love. But you went, said the HuldreFolk. Yes, I went, I said, and when I arrived out East I immediately sought out special places of wildness, trails in the north Georgia mountains and places off the Carolina coast where I learned to sea kayak. So you found wild places there, too, said the HuldreFolk. Yes, I said. I did.

And now you are back here, said the HuldreFolk. Yes, I said, and you are here with me, but you are not all from here, you are not all resident in this particular wilderness area. No, said the HuldreFolk, but our elders live here, some of the ancient ones, and it is good to visit. We are fond of this place, as are you, and we were pleased to know of your fondness and your memories. But we also wanted to remind you that you can find wild places everywhere. There are places that will speak to your heart and become strong in you, they said. Those places are strong for us, too. Find those places, and remember them.

*

The pandemic was receding for a while, at least in America, and people were starting to go out and socialize more. But over all this time so many troubles continued, from wars to social justice protests to insurrection. So much anger and hate and ignorance. I asked the HuldreFolk one night about this strife, which seemed to be occurring across the globe. Why are humans so troubled, I asked, especially as compared with the rest of the natural world. I find it hard to understand.

Don't be too harsh, said the HuldreFolk. Look at the whole of human behavior instead of just the disappointing or recent aspects. It is indeed hard to understand, but you need to take the larger view, if not the longer view. Well, I know there is kindness and intellect and compassion out there, I said, but there is also so much ignorance and anger and hatred. So many lies. Hard to see whether good or evil will prevail.

Look for balance, said the HuldreFolk, and look to the natural world. I don't see any balance, I said, and frankly the natural world also displays extremes…predator, prey; eat or be eaten. That does not seem like a balance that could bring calm to human behavior. The natural world can indeed be harsh, said the HuldreFolk, but it is honest – in the natural world there is no time to hate and no value in being angry, since that only leads to distraction and confusion.

Have patience, said the HuldreFolk. Remember we are earth spirits. The animal spirits are our kin, as they are yours, but earth spirits have more patience than all of you. Good point, I said, but the earth speaks with violence, too, from earthquakes to volcanos to landslides. Yes, said the Huldrefolk, but none of that is done in anger, or in response to a human behavior. It is similar with the animals. The predator – prey relationship you speak of is not one of anger, it is simply part of a balance, one that works in their world.

Humans too often seek the edge of things, said the HuldreFolk, the extreme. The center is a place of balance, not the edge. You know that not that long ago you humans thought the world was flat. You went in search of the edge of your world, fearful that you would fall off but at the same time desperate to find that edge. Instead you found a circle, said the HuldreFolk, a round planet. When you find the center of a circle there is no best direction to go, no distance to be gained from one path to another. Some humans eventually realize that you find balance not at the edge of things, but at the center of things, said the HuldreFolk.

*

Time passes, as it does. It had been weeks since the HuldreFolk last visited and instead I was having unpleasant and troubling dreams related to the pandemic and to suffering generally. Then one night the HuldreFolk appeared again. I told them how relieved I was to see them, that I missed our discussions and found their absence unsettling. We have been here, they said, but we have little control over how or when people hear us or see us in dreams. How can I better ensure that I do hear you and see you in dreams, I asked, because I do not enjoy these other dreams. Just do what you already know how to do, they said. Go for a walk, touch the earth, do a kindness. And just breathe, they said, pay attention to breath. Breathing is so much more of a blessing than most people ever realize, said the HuldreFolk. Take a walk, and just breathe. When I awoke I found myself breathing slowly and deeply, which made me smile.

*

The HuldreFolk returned the next night and said they were glad I took their advice. Humans have constructed a reality for themselves that does not exist for most other living things, they said; you are all too self-important and you forget the most essential things. If you remembered the most essential things you would be more happy, they said, and the world around you would be better.

How can we find more peace and reason in our lives, and in our dreams, I asked. We have already explained that to you, they said, and you already know it in any event. Touch the earth, be kind…and pay attention to your dreams, whether good or bad; learn from them. Dreams are wispy things, said the HuldreFolk, but they are worth remembrance. A few moments in sleep may span years in a dream, but dreams are real, even if they do not reflect reality. Dreams can have impact on your waking lives, said the HuldreFolk. Sleep on it, you will see.

*

One night I asked the HuldreFolk in dreams if they had any thoughts about religion. In response (and in their typical circular fashion) they asked what I meant by the question. Well, I said, humans have many religions, most of which present some idea of a supreme being that offers comfort but expects certain practices to be followed. The HuldreFolk remained silent. I was wondering if any of that resonates with you, I asked, or perhaps the ideas of animism or pantheism, both of which are often likened to religion.

The HuldreFolk asked me to explain animism and pantheism, so I said that animism is thought to be a 'rudimentary' form of religion, where all objects and animals – not just humans – are believed to be infused with spirit, to be spiritual beings. Pantheism is similar, I said, but believes all animals and objects are suffused with the same spirit, while animism sees different beings as having differing spirits. All of these things – religion, animism, pantheism --- are systems of belief.

The HuldreFolk were quiet for a bit, then said we have discussed this before. We do see all things as having spirit, said the HuldreFolk, even if not exactly the same spirit. But no one must believe in us or in other spirits to establish our existence, they said. You only need to see us, and we are around you every day. It is a matter of looking more than a question of belief.

*

The pandemic was returning for another year, bringing sadness, sickness and death again. Bringing social distancing and lockdown again. The HuldreFolk asked me one night if I was lonely, going back to distance and lockdown. No, I said, surprising myself a bit with the ready answer. I am used to being alone, I said, and I have always preferred quiet over crowds. Plus, I have lived a long and interesting life. Those things make it easier to slow down and be quiet.

*

In dreams one night, while walking with my HuldreFolk companion, I told it about a demonstration I had seen recently, where three generations of American Indian women were showing local native plants and explaining their food uses. The mostly non-Indian audience listened politely, but asked repeatedly what the scientific names were for the various plants. Not surprisingly, the women knew and gave the scientific names, along with native names for the plants, which were often multiple for different times of the year. As the small crowd thinned out, one of the women smiled and said that they really didn't pay that much attention to names. She said what they teach their children instead of or in addition to the names was how and where the plants lived, where they could be found at different times of year and in different weather. What trees and birds would be seen where such plants lived, what the winds were like. The purpose being to provide a broader context to the plant's life. The HuldreFolk smiled and said that was a very wise woman, and that of course HuldreFolk are known to traditional peoples. They have different names for you, though, I said. Yes, said the HuldreFolk, but as you have learned the names are not as important as is simply seeing the world as it is.

*

My dogs I and walk every day, several miles every day. We acknowledge the HuldreFolk as we walk, and we talk with the Ravens and Coyotes and Sky around us. Society has changed. I have changed. My thoughts of travel and visits to museums and music venues and plays all were tabled. That was several years ago now. I doubled down on being a recluse, since that is what was presented to me, and because it came naturally. And I found these conversations with the earth spirits helpful.

*

I will pause for now. I should note that I sense the HuldreFolk around me in the daytime now, as well as in dream. They are with me in the waking times. It gives me comfort to know that. It should give you comfort, too. The HuldreFolk encourage me to remind you of what you already know: be kind, touch the earth and remember your dreams.

Printed in the United States
by Baker & Taylor Publisher Services